Before You Start Banking

Please direct any inquiries to:
beforeyoustartbanking@gmail.com

Or call: (773) 231-0729

Purpose

The purpose of this book is to provide insight into the nuances of credit and personal banking for the younger members of society. I highly encourage people to use banking services, but you need to be equipped with the correct information before you sign ANY financial contract. As the leaders of their generation, it will be extremely beneficial for them to learn about banking and credit. This will serve as a mini-guide to the youth, and their caretakers, for money management. In the next few years, they will be offered necessary products to establish credit. The mishandling of debt can haunt someone for years. If you want to become an entrepreneur, get a good job, buy a house, or own a car, you will either need loads of cash, established credit; and in some cases you may need both.

There are so many different pieces to the banking puzzle, but I will stick to personal banking. We will address how banking works, how banks make money, how to manage credit, the importance of good credit, and some do's and don'ts of managing finances. This book is not about getting rich overnight. Savings and investments are a good way to obtain wealth over time, but avoiding temptation to overspend for the things that you want and need is also a part of the formula. There have been many multi-millionaires that have ended up broke and/or bankrupt because of poor financial management and bad financial decision-making. Regardless of how much money you make, your money always needs to be managed properly.

Parents have conversations with their kids about drugs, sex, and getting an education, but discussing credit is equally as important. The reason that many young people have damaged credit, is because they are uninformed, which is no fault of their own. However, what you don't know can hurt you. I do not want to see our youth get taken advantage of, and continuously fall victim to predatory lending. I want to be a resource to ensure that you understand the importance of money management and credit. The best gifts that we can give our youth are love and knowledge.

R. *Williams*

My Story

As a manager in banking for many years, I have seen that many people have not been fully educated to the workings of the banking system. Everyone in this country wants to experience all of the best things the world can provide. For many, living the American dream means having a lot of money in the bank, owning a lavish mansion, and driving one of the world's best cars. Having those aspirations are perfectly fine, within your means. In many cases people overspend to have what they want, which I have been guilty of before.

I found out about the importance of credit the hard way. Once I turned eighteen, I got a few credit cards, worked a part-time job, and went to school. My first credit card was given to me at a booth with t-shirts, pens, and pencils to anyone that filled out an application. One week later, I received the card and went to a party that weekend, taking out a cash advance. I got the windows tinted on my car. It was one of the nicest cars that a teenager could have. Everything was paid for on credit. Once I spent a certain amount, the lender increased my limit from $500 to $1,000. Next week, another credit card company came, and I got another card with a $500 limit. I then applied for another, figuring I couldn't have too many. I got approved for that as well with a $750 limit. I felt cool. I used them as much as I wanted, and I got points for spending so much. I could redeem my points for cash, prizes, and electronics, among other things. I made sure to make the minimum payments every month on time.

The free spending backfired on me big time. I was involved in a car accident sometime later after I lost control in the rain. The accident was my fault. I had a $500 dollar deductible on my insurance policy, but I did not have the money to pay it. Naturally, I applied for another credit card. In the time that I needed money the most, I could not get it, and was declined. I had too much credit. My only option was a payday loan (an advance one can receive against their next paycheck) but I could not get it due to the differing addresses on my driver's license and my checks. I was stuck, and my finances went into a downward spiral. My car was totaled and I still had to pay that $500 deductible. My insurance company threatened to send it to a collections bureau, but thankfully my grandmother loaned the money to me. However, I still had $2,250 in credit card debt to pay back, most of which was put into making my car look nice. Since I had no car, I couldn't get to work. The job was too far away and not accessible by public transportation. I was back to square one. The credit card companies would not work with me, so it damaged my credit report for some time.

With effort, I was able to get a job within walking distance as a bank teller. Working there helped me in many ways. I was able to finally get back to a steady job, collect a paycheck and chip away at the bills. I paid my credit card bills back one by one, but I had to do settlements, where you pay a lower amount to clear up the debt. I was not aware of what I was getting myself

2

into. I had been working at my job for a while and they wanted to transfer me to another branch, but I had a problem; no way of getting there.

I went to a car dealership and I saw a car that I liked, but the payments were out of reach. At the last minute, my mom stepped in and told me not to buy it. I'm glad she did. I was able to get a car in cash with her assistance without paying a car note. This was the day that I truly learned how credit works. The knowledge was appreciated, but it came too late, as my credit was already damaged. I had a friend that was a very accomplished mortgage broker. I had him pull a copy of my credit report. He looked at my credit report and said, "Your credit isn't good. You have a 560 credit score. But, I could get you in a house." I was shocked. I could get a house? He quickly brought me back to earth. "But you will get smacked on your rate. People with good credit always have good options. I deal with people that don't have many options."

As I continued my career in banking I was able to move into a management position. I learned how banks operate internally and the relationship people have with money. I learned how careless I was when I was young, and how important credit really is. I always found myself working in low-income areas, where often I found myself educating many, young and old, about how the bank works and the importance of credit. I have seen many unable to obtain the things that they want or pay higher rates than they had to based on the limited options they had available to them. They were just like me, struggling to repair credit that took a beating when they were young. There's no need for you to pay sky-high interest rates for the things that you want or need. I want you to know that you have options. But, also know that your personal decision-making can easily influence your financial situation.

Intro to Banking

Different components of banking include:

- Commercial – Business Banking
- Merchant Services – Payment Processing
- Treasury Management – Asset Protection and Services
- Wealth Management/Private Banking – Services for the Wealthy

This book will focus on the personal banking aspect of money management. I will explain the different products that someone at a bank may offer you.

Types of banking products

Checking/Savings accounts

A checking account is also known as a Demand Deposit Account or DDA. A bank may offer multiple types of checking accounts based on balances or the services that you use. A checking account is an excellent way to help you manage your money.

Savings accounts are just that. They usually pay more interest than checking accounts, but you will not get checks or a debit card. Money market savings with check writing ability may be the exception. Savings accounts usually have a balance requirement, and you may only be allowed to do a certain number of withdrawals in a predetermined period of time without paying a fee.

Certificates of Deposit

Certificates of Deposit (CD's) are products that banks offer to help you earn interest. A CD will have a specified term or length of time that you must leave your funds on deposit without withdrawing from it. There are numerous terms that you can pick from, but usually the longer the term, the higher the rate.

Debit/Credit Cards

Banks offer debit and credit cards that you can use to purchase items without using cash. Debit cards deduct the funds directly from your checking account, while credit cards will post to your credit balance. Credit cards have an established limit. Debit cards are only limited by your checking account balance.

Safe Deposit Boxes

A safe deposit box is a way for you to place important or valuable items in a safe place, accessible by a set of keys. There are fees associated with the rental. You will also pay a fee if you lose your keys.

Loans

Banks offer many types of loans for many different purposes. Loans are classified as secured and unsecured. The repayment of the loan also depends on if the loan is an installment loan or a revolving loan. I will explain the difference throughout the book. All loans must be paid with interest. Interest is the additional amount that you must repay with the original loan amount. Interest is usually given at a percentage rate, such as 9.99%.

Deposits made into checking accounts, savings accounts, money market accounts and CD's are secured by the Federal Deposit Insurance Corporation (FDIC). Currently, the FDIC will insure your total deposits into the bank up to $250,000, per bank. So, if your bank goes out of business and you have $50,000 deposited into a checking account, you will still be entitled to receive that $50,000 back. For additional information about the FDIC, consult your bank or visit www.fdic.gov.

How do banks earn money?

Banks are "FOR-PROFIT" financial institutions overseen by the FDIC. Banks earn revenue in many different ways, but the main methods are in fees and interest rate spread. When you open a bank account, there are different types of fees of which you may be accountable for.

Monthly Fees

If you have a bank account you may be assessed a monthly fee. Some accounts may allow you to waive the fee if you meet certain criteria. A few examples include having a high balance, using direct deposit, enrolling in electronic statements, or having an E-account. E-accounts mean that you will only use electronic banking. With this account, you may be charged if you see a teller.

Negotiable Item Fees

A negotiable item is when you exchange cash for a paper form of currency. This includes money orders, cashier's checks, and traveler's checks. You may be assessed a fee for purchasing a negotiable item.

ATM Fees

This includes charging customers to use their ATM if they do not have an account with that bank. Please note, if you go to another bank's ATM, you may be assessed a surcharge from your financial institution as well as the machine.

Service Fees

Any time you need to use a service that the bank offers, you may be assessed a fee. Examples include:

- Check reorders
- Check cashing
- Copies of checks or statements
- Early closeout fee
- Notary services
- Overdraft fees / Continuous
- Returned checks
- Stop payments
- Wire transfers – domestic and international
- Other business services

Spread

Spread, or rate spread, is another way that banks make money. When you deposit money in an account, your financial institution will pay you interest on your money, depending on the type you have. A good example of an interest-bearing product is a CD. CDs will pay you a fixed interest rate for an indefinite period of time.

For example, let's say you have $1,000 and the bank is offering you 3.25% Annual Percentage Yield (APY) on a 12-month CD. This means that you will increase your one thousand dollars by 3.25% in twelve months to $1032.50. However, if you withdraw money from your CD before the term ends, you will be assessed an early withdrawal fee. The fee varies, but you may lose a portion of your interest, and possibly a portion of your principal.

With that $1,000 that you put into a CD, the bank will take that money and use it to make additional funds.

Spread scenario: You put $1,000 into a CD that pays 3.25% in twelve months. In return, the bank may take that $1,000 and lend it to a customer in the form of a personal loan or a credit card. Depending on the customer, the interest rate could be anywhere from 5.99% to 19.99% depending on their credit history. If the financial institution takes your $1,000 that they pay you 3.25% interest on and they lend it to a customer who needs a loan for $1,000 at 9.99%, the bank will make a spread on that $1,000 of 6.74%, or $67.40, minding that you do not withdraw your money early, and the person does not pay the loan off in advance.

	1000	Your Investment
*	9.99%	Lending Interest Rate
	$1,099.90	Cost of Loan

	1000	Your Investment
*	3.25%	CD Rate APY
	$1,032.50	Value of CD

	1099.9	Cost of Loan
−	1032.5	Value of CD
	$ 67.40	Spread Profit

The better your credit is you can expect to see lower interest rates. The higher the interest rate means more money out of your pocket, and more money for the bank.

Credit History

The most valuable tool that you can have, even if you have a lot of money, is a good credit report. It is an assessment or rating of how financially responsible you are. My aunt told me that having bad credit is the world's way of telling you that you don't deserve to have what you want. It tells the world that you don't pay your bills, and that you don't know how to manage your own money. Now that I am older I understand. When you obtain credit, they don't get to know some important things about you, such as:

- Who you are
- The quality of your character
- Your involvement in the community
- How much you do for others
- Your good grades
- How you provide for your family
- Awards you've won
- Your passions and hobbies
- Your common sense

Credit bureaus and banks do not have a lot of information about you. They do not know if you had a criminal record as a juvenile or an adult. But, they also do not know if you were the high school valedictorian.

There are four different credit bureaus: Innovis, Equifax, Trans Union, and Experian. Whenever you apply for a credit product from a lender or a creditor, such as a credit card, loan, or a mortgage, they will request copies of your credit reports. They are looking to see proof that you are financially responsible and answers to questions such as:

- Do you pay your bills on time?
- Do you have too much credit?
- Are you using too much credit?
- Do you have any negative accounts?
- Do you have a lot of credit inquiries?

You want your credit report to reflect the best information about you. For all or some, an unforeseen event compromises your credit. The credit bureaus do not know you personally, so they will continue to report anything positive or negative about your financial history. This is why managing your credit is so essential, especially in this economy. There was a time that someone with a credit score of 500 could get approved for a house. However this is not the case anymore. Depending on the lender, people with a 700 credit score and above are usually given good deals.

What affects your credit history negatively?

Late Payments

The easiest way to show financial responsibility is to pay your bills on time. One late payment is the easiest way to decrease your score, even if you are keeping low balances.

Having high balances on credit cards

When you have high balances, this poses a risk that you may be having financial difficulty. When a lender runs your credit report to see your credit history, they look at your current balances. High credit balances on revolving credit accounts may pose a risk.

Collection Accounts

Accounts that are delinquent for too long can end up on your credit report. Collections will not show anything but negative information. Keep track of your bills.

Too many credit inquiries

Trying to obtain too much credit poses a risk as well. Only let someone pull your credit when you need to.

Bankruptcy

Bankruptcy is a last option for people when they just cannot manage their finances anymore. While bankruptcy may be a new start for many people, it is detrimental to your credit history.

Foreclosure

In the current housing crisis, there are many people that have had to involuntarily or voluntarily foreclose on their house. Foreclosure will have a severely negative impact to your credit history. Anytime you apply to purchase another house, lenders will look to see if you have had a foreclosure in your credit history.

Child Support

Yes, people that are behind on child support run the risk of having this reported to the credit bureaus.

Repossession

Anytime that you have had a car, home, or property repossessed, even if you pay the fees to get your asset back, it will still report as a repossession on your credit history. The next time you go to finance something (especially a car) they will look to see if you have had a repossession.

Using too much credit

Having high balances and too many credit products poses a threat as well. In this case, a lender may decide to decline your credit application due to overuse of credit.

A representative from a credit card company will soon approach high school graduates once they enter college, if they have not already. Expect to be contacted within the first week of college by a representative. They make it so appealing to get a credit card because they have a lot of nice things to give away and the application is easy to complete. They will also tell you that it is essential to begin to establish a form of credit. I believe that establishing credit is important, so I will tell you that you should get one, and only one, credit card once you have been in school for a while. Get used to transitioning from high school to college first. There is no need to put more of a burden on yourself than you need to. Your first credit card will probably be a basic credit card with a 0% introductory period, no annual fee the first year, and no set-up costs. Once you are past the introductory period, you can expect to have a double-digit interest rate with an even higher rate for cash advances. Remember that any type of credit must be repaid, so make sure that you will be able to make your monthly payments.

Once you have adjusted to college, you should go to a bank and speak with a banker or a manager about the credit card. Tell them who you are and ask any questions that you have. Bankers are not mind-readers, but they are wells of information for you and will help in any way they can.

Different types of loans

Installment vs. Revolving

Installment loans are loans in which you are required to make a minimum payment each month for a specified period of time, also known as a term. Examples of installment loans are mortgages, auto loans, and student loans.

Revolving loans are loans in which you have a specified credit limit that you may use, such as a credit card. If you have a $1,000 limit but you keep only a $100 balance, you only pay interest on the $100 balance. Other forms of revolving loans are personal lines of credit and home equity lines of credit. With revolving debt, you only pay interest on what you use, but there may be an annual fee on your line of credit.

Unsecured vs. Secured

Unsecured loans can be classified as a personal loan, personal line of credit, credit card, or any other type of loan that is not attached to a piece of collateral.

Secured loans are loans that are attached to a piece of collateral like a house, car, boat, motorcycle, or other property. When a secured loan is complete, the person or business will sign some paperwork allowing the bank to place a lien on the collateral. This lien protects the bank if the customer ceases to make payments on the loan, allowing the bank to recover the collateral. Once the financial institution recovers the collateral, they will make you pay what you owe, plus additional fees to receive the collateral back. If you do not or cannot pay the amount that you owe, the bank will recover the asset and try to resell the collateral to another interested buyer.

When applying for an unsecured or a secured credit product, banks may look at certain financial ratios based on your credit history, your collateral, and your income. Three important ratios are:

- LTV & CLTV – Loan to Value and Combined Loan to Value
- DTC – Debt to Credit Ratio
- DTI – Debt to Income Ratio

LTV & CLTV – Loan to Value and Combined Loan to Value

Anytime you are trying to obtain a secured loan, you must have a source of collateral. The collateral may be a house, car, boat, motorcycle or another financial instrument, such as a CD. An expert will look at the collateral and give it a value. This is known as an appraisal. Based on the reported value of the appraisal on the collateral, the bank will determine if your collateral is good enough for you to take out a secured loan.

Example: If you are trying to purchase a home for $180,000, but it is appraised to be worth $200,000, your LTV = 90%.

To calculate the LTV/CLTV, use this formula:

Amount of total loans or liens/Value of the property - $180,000/$200,000 = 90% LTV

If you are trying to take out multiple loans on the same piece of property, the bank will use the same formula to determine your CLTV.

Example: A house worth $200,000 has a first mortgage for $150,000 and a second mortgage for $30,000. The CLTV is 90%, using the formula below.

To calculate the LTV/CLTV, use this formula:

Amount of total loans or liens/Value of the property

Total loans - ($150,000 + $30,000) = $180,000

Value of the property = $200,000

$180,000/$200,000 = 90% CLTV

The lower the LTV or CLTV the better.

DTC – Debt to Credit Ratio

Anytime you are applying for credit, banks may review your debt to credit ratio. This ratio looks at your credit limits and how much credit you are using. The lower the DTC the better. If your credit limit totals $10,000, but the current balances that you have equal $6,500, then your DTC equals 65%.

To calculate the DTC, use this formula:

Total balances/Total Credit Limits - $6,500/$10,000 = 65%

Try to keep this number at or below 50% at all times. If your debt to credit ratio is too high, this may negatively affect your credit, the bank may view your DTC as a risk, and you may be denied credit or charged a higher interest rate.

DTI – Debt to Income Ratio

This is a ratio that banks look at to ensure that you can afford to make the purchase. Banks will total up all of your monthly payments that are listed on your credit reports, plus the amount for your rent, unless you own your house. Liabilities include student loans, credit card debt, auto loans, personal loans, mortgages, and any other forms of monthly credit. If you own your house, it will show up as a mortgage on your credit report. If your total liabilities are $1,000 per month, but your total income is $4,000 per month, then your DTI is 25%. The lower the DTI the better.

To calculate the DTI, use this formula:

Total liabilities/Total Income – 1000/4000 = 25%

Not included in liabilities are phone bills, cable bills, gas, electric, water, medical bills, and car insurance. If you are to become delinquent on these bills, you might be reported to a collection agency, and they may report your delinquent balance to the credit bureaus. Any collection accounts negatively affect your credit.

Managing your credit

The first key of managing your credit is to only obtain the credit that you can afford. Companies must budget their expenses and costs in order to complete big projects, such as purchasing a new facility, adding a new product line, or purchasing another company. Households need to have this same mentality. Before you can purchase that BMW or purchase that 5,000 square foot house, look at your budget. If you feel that you are spreading your funds too thin, do not do it. The risks far outweigh the rewards in this instance.

The next key to managing your credit is to keep your balances as low as possible. Paying your bills on time is essential, but if you can keep the balances low, you will not pay as much in interest and you keep a safety net anytime you need to use credit for something important.

The next key to managing your credit is to only use what you need. I say this because many people overextend themselves. You keep yourself from paying more in interest and finance charges than you have to if you only use what's necessary. When the unexpected occurs, you have a backup plan.

I remember when I had two customers, a young woman and an older gentleman. Both wanted to purchase luxury cars at the same time. The BMW that she wanted was three years old and had almost 50,000 miles on it. The car he wanted was less than one year old and had 4,500 miles on it, so it was still considered to be a new car. Usually, any car with less than 5,000 miles is considered to be brand-new. She made more money than he did and had more credit history, but had a few old collection accounts. He had three good accounts with no late payments and a credit score nearly 150 points higher than hers. He got a new car and his payments were $230 dollars per month less than what she was approved for. She also had to take the loan out for 12 months longer than he did. After everything was complete, she paid over $16,000 more for an older car than he did. Was this a smart decision? No, she stretched and overpaid to get a car than she didn't need. Although she got the "better model" once I looked at the features of the two cars, the lady's had a bigger motor but had lower miles per gallon. Months later, she came to me because she needed additional money for some business repairs. She was declined. Why? Overuse of credit. Making smart purchases is one of the best ways of managing your credit.

An example of smart purchasing is buying a new electronic item that you need. A new high-demand electronic item is about to be released tomorrow. This device will make it easier for you to organize your life. You want it but do not have all of the money needed to purchase it. You go to a retailer and you notice that if you sign up for their credit card, you may be free of interest for twelve months with discounts on your purchases. You sign up and you are approved for a $1,000 credit limit, which is enough to buy it. The total of the purchase is $500. To pay this off in twelve months, you need to pay $42/month to avoid paying interest, which is the ideal solution. This is an example of using smart purchasing, using credit wisely, and getting what you want without overpaying. The same methodology applies to purchasing nearly anything on credit, including: cars, houses, travel tickets, and other expenses.

Why is keeping a good credit history essential

The first reason is to prevent you from spending more than you have to on the things that you want. It's human nature to want fine things in life, the American dream. The biggest bargaining tool that you have is your credit. When you have good credit, good income, and some money in the bank, you have options. You can pick the best deal, not the only deal offered to you. Let's look at an example. If you plan to purchase a house for $200,000 over thirty years with an annual percentage rate (APR) of 6.25%, the principal and interest payment will be $1,231.43. If you plan to purchase a house for $200,000 over thirty years, with an APR of 4.25%, the principal and interest payment will be $983.88.

	$1,231.43	Principal & Interest Payment 30 Yr. Mortgage at 6.25% APR
-	$983.88	Principal & Interest Payment 30 Yr. Mortgage at 4.25% APR
	$247.55	Savings per month
*	360	Number of Mortgage Payments
	$89,119.66	Total Savings after thirty Years

Your credit history will determine the rate that the lender is going to pre-qualify you for; the better the credit, the lower the rate. Most mortgages are thirty years long, and on a $200,000 house, a two percent difference in the interest rate could save you almost $90,000. That money could be used for retirement, vacations, home improvements; whatever you like. This is a perfect example of how you can have what you want without overspending for it.

The Unexpected

Another benefit of good credit is to have access to additional credit or funds when you need it. More often than not, the unexpected happens when you least want and expect it to. Best believe it, something unexpected WILL happen. You need to be prepared mentally and financially. Things happen and it's unadvisable to reach into your savings account all of the time if you have one. You may need to take out an additional loan or line of credit in order to cover all of your bases. I certainly did not wake up one morning planning to have a car accident.

Whatever the circumstances, you need to be prepared. If you need to obtain credit and your credit history is unsatisfactory, you will probably be declined or pay an enormous interest rate. This may also involve going to a check cashing store, currency exchange, or an auto title loan company. I suggest that you use these places as an absolute last resort. Some of the interest rates on these loans are above 100%. There are many people that use this option on a frequent basis, contributing to financial decline. I've seen people come to the bank to withdraw money from their paycheck, then go to the payday loan store to pay their loan off, then immediately take out another one. The fees associated with payday loans are substantial, with the risks far outweighing the rewards.

Sudden unemployment is another obstacle you must consider. When some people lose their job, their bills fall behind quickly. If you have too much credit that you were struggling to pay, then your credit history may take a big hit. However, if you have kept your finances in check, you may be able to sustain your normal living standards based on your savings, unemployment checks, and/or other income.

Lower Stress

When you are stressed, your body is not the same. Stress can cause high blood pressure, heart attacks, weight gain, and numerous other health-related issues. Financial issues can cause strain in relationships and vastly increase stress levels.

Insurance Policies

There are different types of insurance policies, including homeowner's, auto, renters, and life insurance. Anytime you apply for one of these policies, you are subject to a credit check. Based on the information from the check, you may be declined based on your credit, or you may even get a discount for having good credit.

Predatory Lending/Avoid being "ripped-off"

If your credit score is low, know that you may be a victim of predatory lending and someone may try to rip you off. Predatory lending is deceptive lending practices. However, not every case of someone being ripped off is considered predatory. As a salesman and a banker, I've seen what some lenders have done to people desperate to get a loan. Example: When you are buying a car, the salesman will ask you about your credit to test your savvy. Never tell them that you have bad credit, even if you do. They will always ask what you can afford. They will present their proposal as a payment that is slightly higher than what you asked for. I've seen people get so excited just to get a loan that they will sign the documents because they are just happy to be approved. Once this happens, you've gotten ripped off. You'll probably end up paying double the sales price once you pay the car off. I've seen this happen to many of my colleagues simply because they didn't know. I don't care how good or bad your credit is, never accept their first offer. Always negotiate.

When you have good credit, salesmen know it right away. They will offer you a good deal, maybe not the best deal, but they know that you can go with any lender and get approved. Still negotiate.

Identity Theft

Identity theft is one of the fastest-rising crimes of the last decade. Criminals have cost people and financial institutions billions of dollars. I have personally been the victim of identity theft and it is not fun. Knowing your credit will let you know when you see something that is abnormal on your credit reports. It can take months or years to clear up the trail of damage left by identity theft. Eleven months passed before my credit was back to normal.

Identity thieves will steal anyone's identity that they can find, even babies. I see more and more cases of young people applying for a credit card or a loan and they are denied because someone has already damaged their credit. When you turn sixteen, I suggest that you have a parent or guardian check your credit right away. You need to know as soon as possible if someone has stolen your identity as a child. If someone has, it could be hard for you to establish any type of account that requires a credit check. If you are going to college and you need personal and private loans, you may be denied. Not having the money that you need may make it difficult to continue your education.

If you suspect that you have been a victim of identity theft, please call the police and the four credit bureaus right away. The sooner that you detect and report the identity theft, the better. The credit bureaus will place a fraud alert on your credit report for a specified period of time and you will be notified if someone pulls the report to establish a form of credit. You will have to acknowledge that the application is okay to complete. When you are familiar with your credit, you will know when something looks unordinary.

Disputes

If you notice that you have been a victim of identity theft, or if your credit report states inaccurate information, you can dispute it. The dispute process is very simple, but you need to have sufficient information to back up your claim. The more information that you have to support your dispute claim, the better you will be. You can dispute anything that you notice is incorrect, such as balances, late payments, collections, and personal information.

You are entitled to a free credit report:

- Once per year (www.annualcreditreport.com)
- If you are denied credit, job, or insurance within 60 days
- If you have been a victim of identity fraud

Employers

Some companies are checking the credit reports of potential employees. From experience, I have seen job offers declined after they have checked the candidate's credit report. You don't need to have perfect credit, but employers do not want to see a disastrous report. In an age in which your privacy is slowly diminishing and the job market is not nearly as good as it was before, you must have an edge on your competition. Understand the viewpoint of the employer. Should they hire someone to manage their money when they can't handle their own? They do not know the real you. You might have a college education, but if you are going to be a member of the workforce, you need to show that you can manage yourself before others.

Housing

I've talked a lot about obtaining a mortgage if you decide to purchase your own home. Nonetheless, there are many property owners that check prospective tenant's credit as well, if you decide that you want to rent a house, apartment, condo, etc. I have seen many cases of people being denied housing because of their credit history. Even if you have proof that you are able to pay the deposit and the first month's rent immediately, the owner wants to be sure that they are accepting a good tenant.

Entrepreneurship

If you decide that you want to start your own business, you will have to have access to funds to properly establish your business, promote it, purchase assets, etc. Your personal credit can easily affect the business that you are trying to establish, even if you have plenty of cash. Starting a business is not an easy thing, and you must have access to funds at anytime for repairs, payroll, down times, paying bills, and the unexpected.

Balancing your checkbook

With the boom of online and mobile banking, people do not balance a checkbook like they used to. I do recommend that you have a way to balance your transactions. You need to have a system in place to keep track of your money. I keep track of my receipts to make sure that every transaction has been deducted from my balance. When I do not have receipts left, then I know that my balance listed online is correct. It is imperative to know your balance since this is your responsibility, not the bank's.

You may notice that you have two balances when you view your account, called available and ledger. The ledger balance shows all of the transactions that have posted to your statement. Your available balance is your ledger balance and also any check card purchases that are being held. Remember that neither balance may include gas purchases or if you left a tip at a restaurant or bar, so you will have to manually deduct this from your available balance until the transaction posts to your statement.

Overdraft fees

Everyone knows someone that has been a victim of the overdraft nightmare. Understanding how transactions are processed and keeping up with your funds is the easiest way to avoid it. Banks are for-profit businesses. They are in business to make money, not give it away. When you overdraft your bank account you are charged fees usually ranging from $10 to $40 per overdraft item.

Why did the bank let the transaction go through? Banks are not mind readers. They only manage your transactions for you; they do not manage your money for you. They want you to overdraw; it's how they get paid. You very well may have had the money in the bank when the transaction went through, but there might be outstanding checks, automatic payments, or gas, hotel, and rental car purchases that still have not come through. Overdrafts can be a real hassle. You are already low on funds and the next thing you know you have a negative balance. One overdraft can cost hundreds to thousands of dollars in additional fees. Please always keep track of your money. If your bank offers it, enroll in a form of overdraft protection. It can possibly save you hundreds of dollars and a lot of stress.

Transaction Processing

POS – Point of Sale

This is when you go to a merchant and swipe your debit or credit card as a payment. Your transaction is either approved or declined.

Pin-Based

Is when you must input your PIN in order to withdraw money from the ATM or to purchase an item. When you do a PIN-based transaction, it is posted that business day.

Electronic

Is an online transaction including funds transfers and online bill payments.

Wire Transfer

It is not the same as a funds transfer or a Western Union transfer. A wire transfer is a transaction in which you move available funds directly into a recipient's bank account. You must have the recipient's routing number or Swift Code (for International wire transfers) along with their account number.

Checks

A check is a written contract for financial payment. When you write someone a check for payment, you are giving them permission to accept that check for the amount listed. Banks will verify the numeric amount and the written amount to make sure they match. If the amounts do not match they may deny the check or process the check based on the written amount.

ACH

An electronic or printed check in which you have authorized a merchant to take money directly from your account. They are creating a check and submitting it to your financial institution for payment. They will process the check and send the funds to the merchant. ACH transactions do not always happen right away.

Knowing the different types of transactions and how they are processed is essential in banking. This is where I have seen customers receive the most overdraft fees because of the way banks process transactions. There are a few transactions that you need to know about, especially when using your debit card. Most banks will tell you to use the credit option at the cash register when using a debit card. This allows you to swipe your card and the bank will hold the funds until the transaction posts to your statement. The debit option is similar to an ATM withdrawal; the funds are deducted from your account and processed that business day. Some banks may charge a small fee each time you use the debit option, so beware. I have provided a few examples for you to see how transactions are processed, especially with a debit card.

Deposits

When you put money into a bank account, it is called a deposit. Depending on the method of deposit used to put funds into an account, could delay the time that the funds will be available for usage. Funds that are electronically deposited such as a wire transfer or a direct deposit will be immediately available for use. Cash deposits are immediately available also, but I do not advise you to deposit cash in the ATM. Those funds may not be made available immediately, because ATM deposits have to be processed manually. Check deposits can vary. There are several factors that could delay how fast your check will be available for use. If you have questions about deposits, ask a teller, banker or a manager for assistance.

Using your card at the gas pump

When purchasing gas at the gas pump, most use the credit option. When you use the credit option, most banks will only place a $1 authorization on your card so you can get the amount of gas that you need. Within two to three days, the bank will take out the rest of the money. This is not like using the debit option, which some pumps do not have available, so please make sure that you are keeping track of your available funds.

Hotel & rental car transactions

Hotel and rental car companies will tell you that they will not send the authorization through until you check out of your hotel or bring the rental car back, which is true, but they are holding a certain amount of your funds in the meantime. The cost to rent a car may be $100, but some will hold anywhere from $250-$500 until you bring the car back. Once the car is returned, you will receive the remainder, but within a specified timeframe.

Hotels are similar. You may pay $200 and they may only hold $200, but if you have ordered room service, used their phone services, drank their coffee, or ordered movies, those transactions will not be deducted from your balance until after you check out. Make sure to deduct these services from your balance and add the additional amount to your bill. Some mistakenly think that these services are included in the price of the room, but usually they are not. It is in your best interest to ask. Save money by leaving your laptop at home if you have a smart phone; especially if you have to pay extra in order to use their internet service or phone. When renting a car or reserving a hotel room, use a credit card; keep your spending money separate from the funds that you need to rent a car or reserve your hotel.

Restaurants

When you go to a restaurant, it is common to pay for your dish with your debit card. Pay attention to the final bill. Some restaurants may process the transaction for the value of the meal or add an additional percentage, anywhere from 10%-20%. Keep track of how much your meal cost, including the tip. If they have overcharged you, call your bank to dispute the final price. If you notice that the transaction was initially processed for the price of the meal, then you will need to manually deduct the amount of the tip from your balance.

Returns

When you purchase an item and then decide to return it, the return does not automatically cancel the transaction, even if you completed both transactions on the same day. If you decide to buy a shirt at Macy's only to see the same shirt at another store for a lower price, it makes perfect sense to purchase the cheaper item. However, when you go back to Macy's to return the item; the return does not cancel out the transaction because the bank has already approved it. The return may take three to five business days before the funds are credited back to you. In this situation, you can try to call the customer service department of their bank or credit union to see if they will remove the authorization. This is not a guarantee, and if your financial institution agrees to remove the authorization they may want to call the store personally to speak to a manager or the representative may ask to see the return receipt.

Saving

Saving money is extremely important, especially in this economy. In your budget you should have a weekly, bi-weekly, or monthly amount that you should save. It is easier said than done, but over the years I have learned that it is possible, especially when you are living well within your budget. For college students it is harder to save, considering the high student loan payments, credit cards, and commuting costs. Entry-level wages in the job market also form another obstacle between you and your savings account.

When you have a good savings account, you are your own bank. Instead of always applying for loans, using credit cards or borrowing money from friends, you can use the funds that you have worked hard for without paying finance charges or interest. Having funds in the bank also helps to easily handle the unexpected. Always have a mix of money in the bank, and credit to use.

Credit clean up

If you have damaged your credit, the world is not over, though it will be significantly harder, and more costly, for you to obtain the things that you need and want. There are different agencies available that offer what is called "credit cleansing," a term for credit counseling or debt consolidation services. These are available to anyone, but the associated fees can be significant. Some lenders view this negatively when trying to obtain a new form of credit. You may have no other option, but knowing this in advance will help you explore all of your options.

Final Respects

Now that you understand the basic technical aspects of banking, such as how they make money and process transactions, I hope that you use this information. Do not sign ANY financial contracts without making sure that you are making an informed decision. Ask plenty of questions so that you are well informed. You can have one overdraft, one bad month, and it could take years for you to regain your once perfect credit rating. When you are not overpaying for the things that you want and need, you can afford to buy other stuff or throw a few more dollars into savings. You cannot solve money problems with obtaining more credit; this may take care of your immediate need, but hurt you in the long run.

I am not here to teach you how to become a wealthy investor. However, you can become wealthy by not spending more than you have to. I believe that you should be able to have what you can afford without making the bank rich in the process. When you pay significant bank fees, you are adding to the profits of financial institutions. Paying high interest rates helps the bank earn higher spreads, which they will take and lend to someone else, or pay it out to their shareholders. The bank works very similarly to a middleman. The services that financial institutions offer are valuable in helping you manage your money, obtaining additional funds, and earning interest on your own money, but when mismanaged, you can pay the banks hundreds in fee revenue. When you overdraw your account or use the services that the banks offer, the banker or manager is not always going to be able to waive those fees.

I had a minor bank account when I was fourteen. I saved some money, but I would spend it when I could. I feel that if someone would've given me this knowledge of credit and how banks work at an earlier age, then I may have made better decisions and been a more valuable member of the community. When the community improves, everyone improves. Building credit is not a short-term gig; it's a long-term trek. Many of our older relatives have had to find out about credit, banking, and finance the hard way. If I can prevent that from happening, you will see how much money that you can save simply by managing your finances wisely.

This book is not intended to deter you from using banks and other financial institutions. Your personal decision-making can easily influence your financial situation. Things happen in life all of the time, so you have to be prepared. If you follow this book and the dos and don'ts, you will have a great start to managing your credit for the rest of your life. I encourage all young adults and teenagers to learn about banks and credit before they begin using it. Credit can be an angel and a devil; it's all dependent on how it is managed.

Banking DO's & Don'ts

Do's	Don'ts
Make informed decisions	DO NOT cosign on a loan to someone you are not married to
Manage your credit the best that you can	DO NOT fall for lottery schemes or accept checks from people that you don't know
Have a system for keeping track of all of your purchases	DO NOT use the ATM to check your balance
Make sure that you understand how transactions are processed	DO NOT obtain and/or use more credit than you need to
Know the difference between ledger and available balance	DO NOT stretch yourself to make purchases that you don't need
Know what services you use that the bank may charge you for	DO NOT deposit money in the ATM if you need to use it right away
Know what the prime rate is for credit products and depository products	DO NOT abuse the payday loan service and/or car title loan service
Do take advantage of your free annual credit report	DO NOT give your PIN to ANYONE
Report any identity theft immediately	DO NOT write checks when you do not have the money
Set your own financial goals and objectives	DO NOT simply trust someone to handle your money for you

Do's

Make informed decisions

This is the most important thing you could ever do. Never sign anything without knowing your terms, rates, and fees. If you feel that something may not be the best decision for you, then don't do it. The pen is mightier than the sword for a reason. It would also be very beneficial to learn how to use financial loan calculators. This can also help you determine what your payments should be based on quoted rates, principal, and terms. If the payment that they are quoting you is significantly higher than what you calculated, then there are probably hidden fees included in your loan amount. Don't get taken advantage of.

Manage your credit the best that you can

Having good credit is the best way to have what you want without overpaying for it. Credit is a depiction of your financial responsibility. Show the best you. Credit protection is a service that I recommend also. It may protect you if you lose your job or cannot make payments. Some credit protection services also help you monitor your credit each month. They usually only charge you for the service based on your balance.

Have a system for keeping track of all of your purchases
This is the easiest way to manage your finances without receiving overdraft charges. Have a system of checks and balances for all of your transactions.

Make sure that you understand how transactions are processed
Know so that you can accurately calculate an accurate balance.

Know the difference between ledger and available balance
They are different and you need to balance the meaning of both.

Know what services you use that the bank may charge you for
You may want to buy a house, car, boat, or motorcycle, so you may need copies. The bank may charge you for copies, and they might directly take these charges from your account. You may also have a monthly fee based on your account type or you may be charged a fee for withdrawing money from a CD too early. Know what fees you can be charged for.

Know what the prime rate is for credit products and depository products
Some interest rates are based on the prime rate, which can help you determine what the going rates are for loan products. Ask a banker for rates if you need to obtain credit. Banks run promotions all of the time. Depending on the promotion, you may be able to take advantage of a great deal.

Do take advantage of your free annual credit report
Once per year, you can view your credit history at www.annualcreditreport.com. This is valuable in maintaining your credit.

Report any identity theft immediately
The sooner you detect it, the lower the damages may be. Check your credit when you turn eighteen.

Set your own financial goals and objectives
You have worked hard to obtain the assets that you have. Set your own goals. That may consist of saving for the future, paying down debt, and/or investing. Don't simply trust someone to make good financial decisions for you with your money.

Don'ts
DO NOT cosign on a loan to someone you are not married to
I've seen this happen time and time again. Once the relationship ends, the payments somehow happen to get paid later and later.

DO NOT fall for lottery schemes or accept checks from people that you don't know

There are so many fraudulent schemes out there that many have fallen victim to. Do not do business with strangers on the internet. They can be compelling but they are only trying to take your money. These criminals prey on young adults and the elderly. Once you send your money via wire, especially overseas, there is no way to recover the money and you will be responsible for repayment.

DO NOT use the ATM to check your balance
Most ATMs operate on a different business cycle and your balance may not be accurate. The best way to know what you have in the bank is to calculate it yourself.

DO NOT deposit money in the ATM if you need to use it right away
If you need to use cash right away, make sure that the cash is deposited with a teller so that the funds are available. Not all ATMs have cash readers. A representative that works there processes ATM transactions. If you make a cash deposit at midnight, it will not be verified until sometime during bank business hours.

DO NOT obtain or use more credit than you need to
Maintaining good credit is the easiest way to have the things that you need without spending too much money. Having too much credit is a risk and you may be declined when seeking additional credit or credit limit increases.

DO NOT stretch yourself to make purchases that you don't need
When you stretch, you can easily fall victim to the unknown. When you only use what you need, you keep from paying more interest than you have to.

DO NOT abuse the payday loan service or car title loan service
They are charging you extremely high interest rates to lend you short-term money. Locations: If you have noticed when you see a check-cashing place, there are usually banks within a one mile radius. They live off of repeat customers.

DO NOT give your PIN to anyone
If someone takes money from your account and you give them your PIN, you will be the one held responsible. Memorize it. I suggest that you do not use your birthday, last four digits of your social security number, or the numeric portion of your address.

DO NOT write checks when you do not have the money
This can result in overdraft fees, returned check fees, early account closure, or check kiting, a form of bank fraud.

DO NOT simply trust someone to handle your money for you
Using a financial planner, advisor, relative, etc., is not always a bad thing. Make sure that you do the correct research on them, and make sure that they understand your long-term financial goals. Their goal is to make money also.